W9-AJP-299

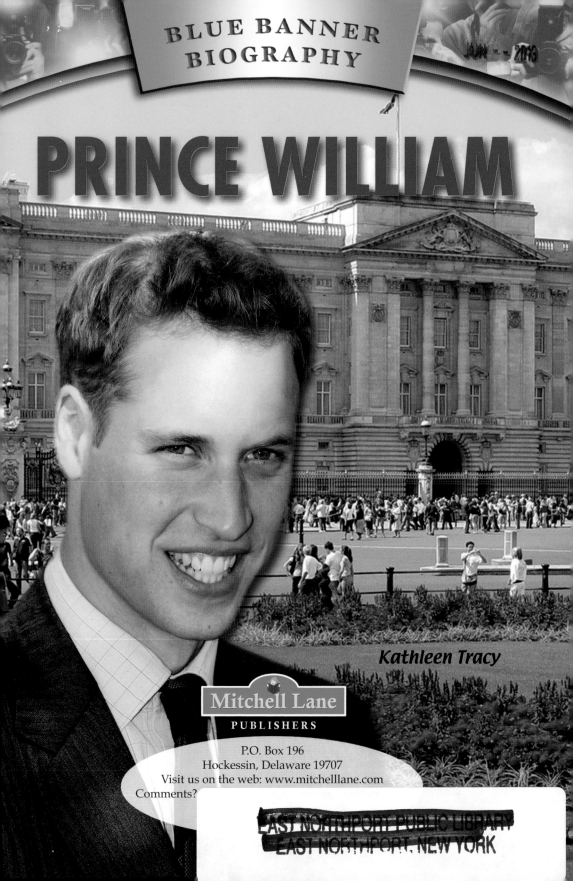

BLUE BANNER
BIOGRAPHY

PRINCE WILLIAM

Kathleen Tracy

Mitchell Lane
PUBLISHERS

P.O. Box 196
Hockessin, Delaware 19707
Visit us on the web: www.mitchelllane.com
Comments?

PUBLISHERS

Printing   1   2   3   4   5   6   7   8   9

Blue Banner Biographies

Alicia Keys	Gwen Stefani	Megan Fox
Allen Iverson	Ice Cube	Miguel Tejada
Ashanti	Ja Rule	Nancy Pelosi
Ashlee Simpson	Jamie Foxx	Natasha Bedingfield
Ashton Kutcher	Jay-Z	Orianthi
Avril Lavigne	Jennifer Lopez	Orlando Bloom
Beyoncé	Jessica Simpson	P. Diddy
Blake Lively	J. K. Rowling	Peyton Manning
Bow Wow	Joe Flacco	Pink
Brett Favre	John Legend	Prince William
Britney Spears	Justin Berfield	Queen Latifah
CC Sabathia	Justin Timberlake	Rihanna
Carrie Underwood	Kanye West	Robert Downey Jr.
Chris Brown	Kate Hudson	Robert Pattinson
Chris Daughtry	Katy Perry	Ron Howard
Christina Aguilera	Keith Urban	Sean Kingston
Ciara	Kelly Clarkson	Selena
Clay Aiken	Kenny Chesney	Shakira
Cole Hamels	Ke$ha	Shia LaBeouf
Condoleezza Rice	Kristen Stewart	Shontelle Layne
Corbin Bleu	Lady Gaga	Soulja Boy Tell 'Em
Daniel Radcliffe	Lance Armstrong	Stephenie Meyer
David Ortiz	Leona Lewis	Taylor Swift
David Wright	Lil Wayne	T.I.
Derek Jeter	Lindsay Lohan	Timbaland
Drew Brees	Ludacris	Tim McGraw
Eminem	Mariah Carey	Toby Keith
Eve	Mario	Usher
Fergie	Mary J. Blige	Vanessa Anne Hudgens
Flo Rida	Mary-Kate and Ashley Olsen	Zac Efron

Library of Congress Cataloging-in-Publication Data
Tracy, Kathleen.
  Prince William / by Kathleen Tracy.
     p. cm. — (Blue banner biographies)
  Includes bibliographical references and index.
  ISBN 978-1-61228-191-9 (library bound)
  1. William, Prince, Duke of Cambridge, 1982– —Juvenile literature. 2. Princes—Great Britain—
Biography—Juvenile literature. I. Title.
  DA591.A45W5585 2011
  941.085092—dc22
  [B]
                                                                              2011021192
eBook ISBN: 9781612281926

ABOUT THE AUTHOR: Kathleen Tracy has been a journalist for over twenty years. She is also the author of over 85 books, including numerous books for Mitchell Lane Publishers, such as *Kelly Clarkson*, *Mariah Carey*, *Megan Fox*, and *Orianthi*. Tracy lives in Los Angeles with her two dogs and African gray parrot.

PUBLISHER'S NOTE: The following story has been thoroughly researched, and to the best of our knowledge represents a true story. While every possible effort has been made to ensure accuracy, the publisher will not assume liability for damages caused by inaccuracies in the data and makes no warranty on the accuracy of the information contained herein. This story has not been authorized or endorsed by Prince William.   PLB

Blue Banner Biography

Prince William trained for nineteen months to become a search and rescue pilot. When he graduated, he said, "I am really delighted to have completed the training course with my fellow students. I absolutely love flying." William is known as Flight Lieutenant William Wales, and he flies a Sea King helicopter.

A Royal Rescue

*T*he weather on Mount Snowdon was getting worse by the minute. Thick fog made it impossible to see more than a few feet ahead. Howling, gusty winds turned the cold rain into icy barbs that stung the skin of the man stranded on the mountainside. What started as a relaxed walk with friends had turned into a life-and-death emergency for Greg Watkins. He had suffered a heart attack, and the weather had suddenly turned as a storm front closed in.

Through the murky haze came the sound of a helicopter. Fighting the wind, lack of visibility, and pelting rain, the pilot maneuvered close enough for the rescue team to secure Watkins and hoist him into the chopper. It wasn't until they were at the hospital that the rescued man realized who the pilot was.

"The winchman helped me out and on to a stretcher and whispered, 'Prince William's just flown you here,' " Watkins recalled in *The Daily Telegraph*. "I looked up at him and just said, 'Oh. Tell him thank you.' How he managed to get the helicopter so close defies belief. He'd probably say he was just doing his job but, to me, he and his crew are heroes."

In public, Prince William is known for being polite, charming, and unassuming. The daring rescue gave people a rare glimpse into William's life as a Royal Air Force (RAF) search and rescue pilot. It's the kind of dashing, courageous image that befits a future king.

> *It was a fairytale romance playing out in real life—and in front of millions of viewers live on television.*

The rescue came just 48 hours after Prince William, second in line to the British throne, announced his engagement to Kate Middleton. Between the two events, William found himself at the center of media attention, a place he has carefully avoided most of his life. The public's interest in and fascination with William and Kate was reminiscent of another wedding that had taken place almost 30 years earlier. . . .

It was a fairytale romance playing out in real life—and in front of millions of viewers on live television. Diana Spencer, a twenty-year-old kindergarten teacher's aide, was marrying Prince Charles, the future king of England.

Their courtship began slowly and privately. On their first date, he invited her to hear a symphony. Then he invited her to lunch at Buckingham Palace. On both occasions, Diana was accompanied by a chaperone. In early September of 1980, Charles invited Diana to spend a weekend at the Balmoral royal estate in Scotland to be formally introduced to his family. Diana stayed with her sister Jane, who lived in a small farmhouse on the estate with her husband.

Charles and Diana spent part of their honeymoon by the River Dee on the Balmoral estate in September 1981.

Charles and Diana spent most of their waking hours together. One day, they went fishing, and while walking the River Dee, Diana noticed some photographers taking pictures of her. She tried to avert her face but it was too late. On September 8, *The Sun* newspaper ran photos of Diana and Charles, making their budding relationship public.

In February 1981, Prince Charles proposed to Diana. She said yes immediately and Charles gave her a diamond-and-sapphire engagement ring. Three weeks later, the engagement was made public. Literally overnight, Diana found herself in a whirlwind. The British press—and public—couldn't get enough of her. Her shyness and down-to-earth demeanor made her very relatable and accessible. She would be the first British citizen to marry an heir to the British throne in 300 years.

In the weeks leading up to the wedding, Diana and Charles' every move was reported in breathless detail. And not just in Britain. All over the world, people were fascinated with the story of the prince and his bride-to-be. They were intrigued by the young girl who would presumably one day be queen. CNN and other news channels prepared to broadcast the wedding live.

The wedding took place on July 29, 1981. Across America, restaurants and bars stayed open all night for viewing parties. It is estimated that 750 million people across the globe tuned in to watch the event.

The wedding took place at St. Paul's Cathedral in London. Diana and her father traveled from Clarence House to the church in a glass coach. The ceremony, attended by 3,500 guests, began at 11:20 A.M., with the Archbishop of Canterbury presiding.

After exchanging their vows, the newlyweds left St. Paul's and rode in a convertible to Buckingham Palace for an intimate reception of 120 family members and close friends. At least 600,000 people lined the streets and cheered the royal

Prince William weighed 7 pounds 1 ½ ounces at birth. As the oldest son of the Prince of Wales, William is second in line to the British throne. His grandmother, Elizabeth II, has been queen of the United Kingdom and 15 other realms since 1952.

couple as they passed. A little after one o'clock in the afternoon, Diana and Charles appeared on the balcony and shared their first public kiss, then went back inside the palace. Later that afternoon, the prince and princess left for a three-month honeymoon. By the time they returned to London at the end of October, Diana was pregnant with the couple's first child. Her pregnancy was officially announced on November 5, 1981, and eight months later, Prince William was born.

To most of the world it seemed that the future heir to the throne would enjoy an idyllic childhood. But by the time Prince William turned eighteen, he had experienced more than his share of personal pain and loss.

William and Harry have a strong bond as brothers. Ever since Harry was born, William has been right by his side. They both learned how to ride horses together at a young age.

A Royal Heir

William Arthur Philip Louis Windsor was born June 21, 1982, in London's St. Mary's Hospital. He was the first heir to the British throne to be born in a hospital. His official title given at birth was His Royal Highness Prince William of Wales. His home was Kensington Palace in London.

Less than two years later, William's brother, Prince Henry, was born. Diana doted on her two sons, whom she called Wills and Harry. She wanted the boys to have as normal an upbringing as possible, so Diana often resisted traditional protocol when it came to her children. For example, she was openly affectionate with Harry and Wills in public, quick to hug or kiss them. By contrast, when Prince Charles was a boy, his mother, Queen Elizabeth, never publicly displayed physical affection. She considered it improper.

Diana also broke tradition when it came to education. She insisted Prince William go to a public school instead of having a private tutor at home, like Charles had as a child. She wanted William to get to play with other children his age. When he was four, he became the first Windsor to go to a public nursery school. He immediately fit in and was popular with his classmates, and he stayed there, at Mrs. Mynors's Nursery School, for two years.

At the same time, William wasn't a typical student. He was the only five-year-old who came to school accompanied by bodyguards. Also, when he traveled, he was not allowed to fly in the same airplane as his dad. That way if there was an accident, only one future king would be lost instead of two.

> **William's best subjects were reading and spelling. Naturally athletic, he was an excellent swimmer.**

Whenever he was in public, William was followed by groups of photographers. At home, Diana made sure he and Harry had some normal fun. They would roller skate down the long palace halls. They had Jelly Babies eating contests. (Jelly Babies are soft candies like Gummi Bear candies.) They would use sheets and dress up as ghosts. Diana also took them to amusement parks and fast-food restaurants. More than any British heir-apparent before him, William was able to enjoy the same experiences regular children did.

William told Matt Lauer on the *Today* show that when they visited Disney World, "Everywhere we went, everyone was really sweet to us. But you know one of the things that [Harry and I] kept sort of joking about was about how many times we were told to watch our heads and mind our step."

After leaving Mrs. Mynors's, William enrolled at the Wetherby School. His best subjects were reading and spelling. Naturally athletic, he was an excellent swimmer. He was also a mischievous six-year-old. And the British newspapers reported every prank. One time, he flushed his dad's shoes down the toilet. Another time, he got into a fight with a flower girl at his uncle Andrew's wedding.

He could be rebellious, too. He once slipped away from a riding lesson while at Balmoral Castle. For a half hour, nobody knew where he was. His grandmother, the Queen, was furious. After that, he was forced to wear an electronic tracking bracelet.

When he was eight years old, Prince William was sent to Ludgrove boarding school, which is 25 miles from London. Initially, Princess Diana was against sending him to boarding school. Prince Charles was equally hesitant because as a

Polo is a traditional pastime of the English royal family. Like his father, William plays polo competitively for the Highgrove Team.

The national sport of the United Kingdom is football, the British term for soccer. William was the captain of his team.

young boy he had been very unhappy at one. But boarding school offered William security, and a compromise was reached. He would attend Ludgrove Preparatory School, but he could come home on weekends.

He shared a room with four other boys. As he got older, William became less rambunctious and more thoughtful. At school, he channeled his energy into sports. He was the rugby and hockey team captain, an excellent shot, a good soccer and basketball player, and participated in cross-country running and swimming.

In March 1991, William made his first official public appearance as a British royal. He visited Cardiff, the capital of Wales, on St. David's Day with his parents. (St. David is the patron saint of Wales.) After touring the city, Prince William met some local schoolchildren, who gave him presents. He accepted their gifts with a smile and a shy thank you.

A couple of months later at school, a fellow student accidentally hit William in the head with a golf club. William was rushed to the hospital, where he was diagnosed with a fractured skull and had to undergo surgery. Fortunately, he recovered fully, although he was left with a scar. Years later, William jokingly called it his Harry Potter scar. "I call it that because it glows sometimes," the BBC reported. "Some people notice it, and some people don't notice it at all."

Even though he missed his brother and parents while at boarding school, William was happy. But within a year, the family life he had known would abruptly end.

> **William was rushed to the hospital, where he was diagnosed with a fractured skull and had to undergo surgery.**

A Broken Royal Home

*I*n December 1992, during William and Harry's holiday break from school, Diana and Charles officially separated. Rumors that their marriage was in trouble had long been suggested in the British newspapers.

After the separation, William and his brother split their time between their parents. The differences in parenting styles became more obvious. When they were with Diana, they could wear jeans. With their father, they were expected to wear jackets and ties.

Diana loved taking William and Harry on great adventures, so they would vacation in the Caribbean or go white-water rafting. Charles preferred spending time with his sons at any of the family estates, where they would go hunting, fishing, or horseback riding.

While Charles helped instill William's sense of duty, Diana wanted him to be compassionate. She would take him to visit the homeless or patients who were terminally ill. In *Diana: A Portrait in Her Own Words*, she says, "I want William and Harry to experience what most people already know. That they are growing up in a multi-racial society in which everyone is not rich, or has four [vacations] a year, or speaks standard English and drives a Range Rover."

Later, William recalled on the *Today* show, "I learned about how she'd always keep an eye on people who worked for her or people she knew who were friends; she always used to keep a little eye on their lives, the ups and downs. She'd always be there on the downs for her friends. She was massively strong like that and gave us both reservoirs of strength."

In 1995, when he was thirteen, William was admitted to Eton College, where he studied geography, biology, and art history. Life at Eton was very regimented. Students had to be up by 8:00 A.M. and were required to attend chapel after breakfast. The rest of the morning was spent going to class. There was a break for sports activities. The fastest swimmer at the school, William was named captain of the swim team. Afterward, the students went to their afternoon classes. The school was close to Windsor Castle, so every Sunday afternoon he would have 4:00 tea with his grandmother. Even so, William says that while growing up, he was not particularly close to his grandparents. As he got older, the relationship improved, especially with his grandfather, Prince Philip.

"He makes me laugh, he's very funny," William told *BBC News*. "He's also someone who will tell me something that maybe I don't want to hear, but still tell me anyway and he won't care if I get upset about it. He knows it's the right

> "She [Diana] was massively strong like that and gave us both [William and Harry] reservoirs of strength."

thing to say and I'm glad he tells me because the last thing I want is lots of people telling me what I want to hear. I'd much rather hear what the reality of it is."

After the separation, Diana was constantly followed by paparazzi. Worried about the media intruding on William's life the same way, the royal family made a deal with the British press. The newspapers would receive information on William once every term in exchange for the papers' respecting his privacy.

"Being in the spotlight is kind of awkward but it's something I've got to do and something I can adapt to."

There were still photographers staking him out, just in case something newsworthy happened. And William was aware of the scrutiny. "You never really grow used to it, because it's something that's very alien to most people," he said on *Today*. "There are very few people you can talk to about it because no one really knows what it's like apart from family, mostly. I'm not really the attention-seeking type. So being in the center of the spotlight is kind of awkward but it's something I've got to do and something I can adapt to."

The lack of privacy made William appreciate his times out of the public eye even more. "I value the normality I can get, doing simple things, doing normal things more than anything, rather than getting things done for me, which I'm not a big fan of."

In 1996 William's parents divorced. A year later, on August 31, Diana was killed in a car accident. In Great Britain and around the world, there was an outpouring of grief for

William and his uncle, Earl Spencer, hang their heads during Princess Diana's funeral. He later said of his mother, "She wanted to give so much love and give so much care to people who really needed it."

Diana, who had become known as the People's Princess. During the funeral, William and Harry walked behind the hearse with their father. Both boys looked shell-shocked. Years later, William admitted that losing his mother was "one of the hardest experiences that anyone can ever endure. Never being able to say the word *mummy* again in your life sounds like a small thing. However, for many, including me, it's now really just a word—hollow and evoking only memories."

He also says the pain of loss doesn't completely go away. "When you knew somebody or someone that important to you, you always think about it. I mean, straight after it happened we were always thinking about it. Not a day goes by when I don't think about it once in the day."

College Years

William completed his studies at Eton in 2000. He took a year off of school to participate in British Army training exercises in Belize. He also went to Chile for two and a half months to tutor children. While there, he lived with other young teachers. During his time off, he volunteered as the guest disc jockey for the local radio station.

When he returned to Britain, William enrolled at the University of St. Andrews in Scotland. Tall and handsome, he had become a kind of teen idol. When news of his plans to attend the college was reported in the press, the university was flooded with applications, many from young women. Initially, William listed his major as art history but later changed it to geography.

At first, William wore hats so that people wouldn't recognize him and bother him, but he soon realized that the local residents weren't paying that much attention to him. In an interview with *BBC News*, he revealed, "In London, . . . people are like, 'Hang on a sec, isn't that someone or other?' But up here it's so good because everyone sees me around the whole time and it's no big deal, which is what I really

William went on an expedition to Chile to help teach English to the children of the village of Tortel. While there, he made friends with ten-year-old Marcela Hernadez-rios, who liked to play soccer.

want it to be. The last thing I want to do is cause loads of hype or problems. I just want to go in there and get my asparagus or whatever. So, it's really worked well."

While at St. Andrews, William says he lived a regular life. "I do all my own shopping. I go out, get takeaway, rent videos, go to the cinema, just basically anything I want to really. . . . There's lots of people saying it's impossible to lead a normal life really but actually up here, and with the media out of it, it's amazing how people just get on with their lives and will not bother you."

While his mother had famously suffered from bouts of depression, William was well adjusted and optimistic. "The thing is with me, I look on the brighter side of everything," he told *BBC News*. "There's no point being pessimistic or being worried about too many things because frankly life's too short. At the moment it's about having fun in the right places, enjoying myself as much as I can. I'm trying to do that. The serious side of that doesn't really need to worry me too much yet."

During his college years, William was considered Britain's most eligible bachelor. But in 2001 during his first year at St. Andrews, he became friends with a fellow art history major named Katherine "Kate" Middleton. The following autumn, William moved into a four-bedroom apartment with her, William's friend Fergus Boyd, and a fourth student. At the time, Kate made light of their living arrangement, saying it was platonic. But others believed Kate and William were a couple.

William (in blue) fends off opponent Eoin Healy in a water polo match for the Scottish National Universities Squad in the Annual Celtic Nations tournament against Wales and Ireland.

While at St. Andrews, William enjoyed more privacy and was able to go shopping for school supplies without much media attention.

Their relationship was made public in 2004 when they were photographed together on a Swiss ski trip. William immediately downplayed the relationship. "Look, I'm only 22 for God's sake," he told *The Sun* newspaper. "I don't want to get married until I'm at least 28 or 29."

In June 2005, William graduated from St. Andrews. The ceremony was attended by his father and his grandparents. William said it was a big day for his family. It was also bittersweet. "I have thoroughly enjoyed my time at St. Andrews and I shall be very sad to leave. I just want to say a big thank you to everyone who has made my time here so enjoyable. . . . I am going to miss being in Scotland."

With his education officially over, it was time for Prince William to assume more royal duties and think about his future. It would be several more years until he was finally ready to settle down, but when he was, it would be worldwide news.

Traditionally, English royals have married for political reasons rather than for love. During their reception, William gave a speech in which he reportedly said Kate is "my rock."

Wedding of the Twenty-First Century

*I*n the summer after his graduation, Prince William went on his first solo royal visits, worked at a financial company, learned about land management on a country estate, and assisted a mountain rescue team. "Joining a mountain rescue team really appealed to me as I can learn at first-hand how these amazing people help save lives on a regular basis," he told *People*. "I very much hope that these work placements will give me hands-on experience in three very different, but important areas."

Early in 2006, William entered Sandhurst, the British Army officer initial training center where Harry was also in training. In early 2008, William spent four months training with the Royal Air Force to learn how to fly helicopters and planes. Specifically, he wanted to work as a search and rescue pilot.

Through it all, he and Kate continued to see each other. Looking back now, William admits, "We went through a few stumbling blocks like any other relationship, but we picked ourselves up. I'm obviously extremely funny and she loves that," he joked to the BBC. "When you go out with someone you go through the good times, the bad times, you can really learn things about yourself."

Finally, in October 2010, after dating for eight years, Prince William proposed while he and Kate were vacationing in Kenya. The engagement was made public in November. Both families expressed excitement that the couple would finally be married.

> After dating for eight years, Prince William proposed while he and Kate were vacationing in Kenya.

In their first televised interview, William says he had decided the vacation was the right time to propose. "We'd been talking about marriage for a while so it wasn't a massive surprise," he said. "We were planning it for at least a year, if not longer. I was carrying the ring around for three weeks in a rucksack before that. And I literally would not let it go, wherever I went."

The engagement ring William gave her had belonged to Princess Diana. He said it was his way of making sure his mother was part of his engagement. He also noted that Kate was not the next Diana. "It's about carving her own future. No one's trying to fill my mother's shoes."

William and Kate were married on Friday, April 29, 2011, at Westminster Abbey. Once again, millions of people around the world watched. William admitted that prior to the ceremony he battled nerves. "I was doing the rehearsals the other day and my knees started tapping quite nervously. It's quite a daunting prospect," *Time* magazine reported.

Approximately 2 billion people caught a rare glimpse of affection between the newlyweds as they kissed twice on a balcony at Buckingham Palace.

More than fifteen hundred British Navy, Army, and Royal Air Force (RAF) military personnel participated in the wedding, providing escorts and music for the royal couple. Instead of wearing his RAF uniform, Prince William wore the red tunic of the Irish Guards for the wedding, representing his honorary position as Colonel of the Irish Guards. Kate Middleton's long-sleeved lace and ivory satin wedding dress was designed by Sarah Burton, long-time fashion designer and Creative Director of the Alexander McQueen brand.

The newlyweds, who were given the titles Duke and Duchess of Cambridge by Queen Elizabeth, enjoyed a festive reception Friday evening that went into the early morning hours. More than 300 close friends and family members attended. In keeping with royal tradition, instead of throwing it, Kate's bridal bouquet was placed on the grave of the unknown soldier at Westminster Abbey.

The newlyweds were not able to take a long honeymoon right away because William needed to return to work as a search and rescue pilot. They spent a quiet weekend at an undisclosed location before returning to Wales. Buckingham Palace announced that for the couple's privacy, plans for their honeymoon would not be made public.

In the summer of 2011, Prince William and Kate planned make their first official overseas trip together, traveling to Canada in June for a nine-day visit. From there, the Royal Couple would spend three days in California. It would be Kate's first trip to the United States and William's first official trip. He would represent the Royal Family as well as Britain's film industry. In 2010, he was named the fifth president of the British Academy of Film and Television Arts (BAFTA). The organization has close ties to the Royal Family, with William's grandfather, Prince Philip, having served as the first president.

> *William expects to be ready when the time comes to be king. "Keeping your feet firmly on the ground is the most important thing."*

As for the future, William says he expects to be ready when the time comes to be king. "The fortunate thing is I have had such a normal childhood in certain extents and it would be very hard to see that slip away. But I always hope that no matter what, I'll keep that side going. Keeping your feet firmly on the ground is the most important thing."

1982 William Arthur Philip Louis Windsor is born June 21 to Charles and Diana, the Prince and Princess of Wales.

1995 Prince William attends Eton College.

1997 Princess Diana is killed in car accident while in Paris.

2000 William works as a teacher in Chile.

2001 He enrolls at the University of St. Andrews in Scotland.

2002 He moves into an apartment with three friends, including Kate Middleton.

2003 His relationship with Middleton becomes public.

2005 William graduates from St. Andrews on June 22.

2006 He enters Sandhurst Military Academy in January, and graduates in December.

2007 William reports for duty with the Royal Air Force in January.

2010 He begins working as a search and rescue pilot in September. On November 16, he and Kate Middleton announce their engagement. William makes his debut as the president of the British Academy of Film and Television Arts (BAFTA).

2011 William and Kate are married in Westminster Abbey on April 29.

Works Consulted

"A Conversation with William and Harry: In Honor of Princess Diana." *Dateline NBC*, June 23, 2007. http://www.msnbc.msn.com/id/19190534/ns/dateline_nbc-a_conversation_with_william_and_harry/t/honor-diana/

"Here Comes Wills." *Time*, Special Report: Princess Diana, 1961–1997, July 22, 1996. http://www.time.com/time/daily/special/diana/readingroom/9697/72296.html

Netter, Sarah. "Pint-Size Interviewer Grills Prince William on Childhood, Scars." *Good Morning America*, March 19, 2009. http://abcnews.go.com/GMA/story?id=7120388&page=1

NewsCore. "UK's Prince William Helps Save Man's Life in Chopper Rescue." *Daily Telegraph*, November 22, 2010. http://www.dailytelegraph.com.au/news/uks-prince-william-helps-save-mans-life-in-chopper-rescue/story-e6freuy9-1225958187465

Perry, Simon. "Prince William Graduates from College." *People*, June 23, 2005. http://www.people.com/people/article/0,,1076369,00.html

"Prince William and Kate Middleton Talk About the Moment, the Ring, Children," *World News with Diane Sawyer*, November 16, 2010. http://abcnews.go.com/Entertainment/prince-william-kate-middleton-interview-transcript/story?id=12163826

Roberts, Laura. "2010: Prince William Becomes President of BAFTA." *Telegraph* [UK], February 21, 2010. http://www.telegraph.co.uk/culture/film/baftas/7287187/Bafta-Awards-2010-Prince-William-makes-his-debut-as-the-president-of-the-Baftas.html

"Transcript: Prince William Interview." *BBC News*, November 19, 2004. http://news.bbc.co.uk/2/hi/uk_news/4026131.stm

Wilkinson, Peter. "Royal Wedding Shows Diana's Influence Lives On." *CNN*, April 27, 2011. http://www.cnn.com/2011/WORLD/europe/04/27/uk.royal.diana.influence/index.html?hpt=C2

"Wills in His Own Words." *Hello! Magazine*, November 22, 2004. http://www.hellomagazine.com/royalty/2004/11/22/williaminterview4/

Books

Doeden, Matt. *Prince William & Kate: A Royal Romance*. Minneapolis, MN: Lerner Classroom, 2011.

O'Shei, Tim. *Diana, Princess of Wales*. Mankato, MN: Capstone Press, 2008.

Tieck, Sarah. *Prince William*. Edina, MA: Big Buddy Books, 2011.

On the Internet

English Monarchy
    http://www.englishmonarcy.co.uk

Flikr: The British Monarchy's Photo Stream
    http://www.flickr.com/photos/britishmonarchy/

The Official Royal Wedding Web Site
    http://www.officialroyalwedding2011.org/

The Official Website of the British Monarchy
    http://www.royal.gov.uk/

The Prince of Wales
    http://www.princeofwales.gov.uk/personalprofiles/

The Royal Air Force Search and Rescue Force
    http://www.raf.mod.uk/rafsearchandrescue/

Time: "Why Princess Diana Mattered"
    http://www.time.com/time/specials/2007/0,28757,1650830,00.html

Balmoral Castle in Scotland